Spirits on the Mountain
A True Story

Aris Govjian

Written, Illustrated, and Published by
Aris Govjian

For my Father, Alex I. Govjian

Contents

Old Bayonets

Introduction

Çatli Samel was an Armenian hero in the westernmost part of the Armenian homeland during the Armenian Genocide, which took place in the heart of Asia Minor during World War I. The Ottoman Empire was crumbling, and the Turkic majority, led by fanatical religious and contrived nationalistic ideology, carried out the first genocide of the twenty-first century.

Yozgat was one of the regions in Turkey populated by a large number of Armenians, including my own family. They lived in the village of Saray Köy located within the highland's mountainous terrain. While their traditions, customs and unique dialect did not survive the genocide, many stories from the time have continued to be passed down through generations. The story of Çatli Samel is one my father has shared with me throughout my life.

Çatli Samel was the last of the fighting Armenians of Yozgat. At a time when nearly all the Armenians in the area were eliminated, Çatli Samel was a rock the Turks could not conquer. The mountain Samel lived on was impossible to overtake, his army too powerful to cripple, his faith too strong to waiver, and resourcefulness too ingenious to surpass.

My family has passed down his story for two generations, and I would now like to share it with you.

Spirits on the Mountain

A Small Village Nestled Near a Forest With Mountains in the Distance

A river of red flows through the villages of Yozgat. In Saray Köy an elderly woman hangs her newly acquired blood stained sheets and brings herself to the home of an Armenian family.

The Armenians are gathered and argue about the horrors they heard. Rumors have spread in the small village. The village patriarch listens carefully to what is being said, looking for a reason to reject what he hears.

The leader's own son, Alexander, came from the Ottoman military a month ago, begging his family and the Armenians to leave, but they thought he lost his sanity at war. Disappointed, Alexander left to find friends who could help. Even in the midst of danger, the Armenians could not imagine how the rumors they heard could be true.

The elderly Turkish woman approaches the Armenians. She has warned the patriarch to flee, and this time she has proof to go with her warning.

She urges their leader Aris to see her new sheets. There is no doubting the truth now. The unimaginable has become real.

Soldiers, along with local Turkish men led by a Cleric gather at Aris' home. The Turks offer Aris and the rest of the Armenians a chance to live, with the condition they raise their children as Turkish and abandon their Christian faith.

The Armenian villagers say to their patriarch they will do whatever he decides to do. Aris says no, he will not abandon who he was born to be. He is an Armenian and a Christian.

The Turkish soldiers fill their military carts with shining yellow gold, rich artwork and culture from the Armenian homes. The Turkish mob takes from the homes and families whatever they can acquire.

A handful of Armenian children, including Aris' little grandson, escape into a nearby forest beneath a mountain's shadow. The forest was their refuge for a time. As Turkish mobs attacked Armenians throughout Yozgat, they hesitated before venturing too deep into the dark garden of trees at the foot of the mountain. Every attempt they made to ascend the summit was met with swift vengeance.

A Forested Path Leads up the Mountain

For nearly half a year Ottoman soldiers attempted to take the mountain, yet every advance turned to defeat. No matter where their cannons fired, or guns began their volley, they could not hit their mark. One by one they would fall.

A forest of dark trees lay stretching out from beneath the mountain's steps with only a cool mist separating the quiet morning from the violent noon.

It was whispered an army of spirits ruled the mountain. The approaching force could not see one Armenian among the ranks, or even eye one rifle. Only white smoke with the sound of gunfire could be seen and heard. This was the army of Çatli Samel.

Though there was a constant Ottoman military presence, the surrounding Turkish towns and villages feared Samel's forces, and so they had little choice but to give him every provision he desired. Samel rode his horse from village to village demanding munitions, food, and supplies and none would resist. He would say "I can bring my army down from the mountain and take much more than what I am asking." This is how he kept his army fed, clothed, and armed. It was easier to give up the little he asked for than to face a threat of an Armenian army.

While the Armenians of Yozgat were largely destroyed, the Turkish villagers and soldiers lived in constant fear of Samel and his army. Samel's presence drew the military's attention away from the hiding Armenians and onto a single futile rock which they could not conquer.

A Little Boy

     As Çatli Samel was riding his horse into town, he saw a six-year-old Armenian boy crying. The child was covered in his own blood. He stopped his horse and asked the child why he was crying. The child said he was alone, and a Turkish man beat him badly. Samel asked the child to show him who. As they approached a large and tall man, Çatli asked if he hurt the child. The Turkish man shouted "Why do you care? He's an orphan!" Immediately Çatli Samel drew his sword and decapitated him.

Wave after wave of Turkish soldiers would charge Samel's mountain, to meet their death. The Ottoman military leaders began to grow restless. Their men quivered in fear at the thought of approaching the mountain, as it offered an assured end to their lives.

The officers began to craft a plan for Çatli Samel, a special deal they could entice him with. They would let him leave his mountain in peace, with the condition he abandons his men, for them to lay down their weapons and surrender. If he agreed, then he could leave the mountain and go wherever he pleased. They would even give him gold and looted treasure.

Çatli Samel and Wife.

Upon a clear day, the orphaned Armenian boy saw Çatli Samel coming down the mountain. This time Samel came with his wife. She was atop the horse and he was walking beside her. Ottoman officers and soldiers were waiting for them outside the forested path. The leading Turkish officer seized him and held him, arm-in-arm as they both began to laugh.

The boy thought to himself how foolish Samel was to surrender and forsake his army. The hiding Armenians who heard the news mourned, having seen others who forfeited their lives when surrendering to a false promise of peace.

It was believed Çatli Samel and his wife suffered a similar fate.

9

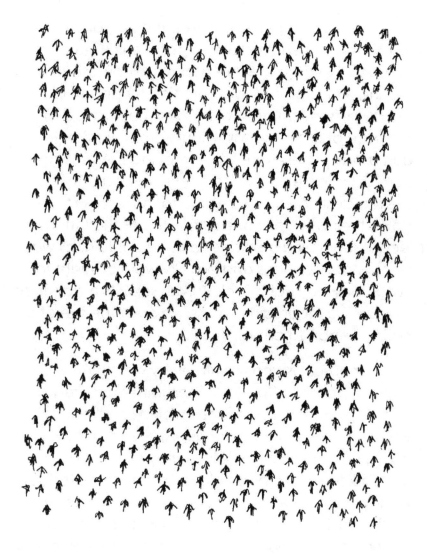

A Forest of Trees

10

Though Samel had surrendered his army, the Turkish forces behaved rather peculiarly. They refused to charge the mountain again. They were waiting. Perhaps they were waiting for approval. Approval from whom? For months they waited at the base of the mountain. Finally, from what one can assume, they received a message. A message from Çatli Samel, who had long since reached his desired destination. It was time for his forces to lay down their weapons and surrender. As the Ottoman leader shouted a message to the mountain, all was silent. More cannons and cavalry were brought to Yozgat for the final attack. Turkish soldiers made their way up the mountain in mass. An army the size of a nation began to climb.

Thousands armed with every weapon Germany could afford marched with fear, dread, and anticipation. Finally, they would see the army which has eluded them for nearly a year. Turkish troops remained breathless as they crept through the dark trees and brush along the mountain's side. At any moment they could be cut down as previous armies had been. As the night's shade began to cover the sky, thoughts of spirits and ghosts bled into the soldiers' minds as they began to shake. Every brush of wind and sound was an omen. Samel might be gone, but his army was still there.

They searched and at last, they found
weaponry. Scattered throughout the ridges of the
mountain were rusted rifles, yellowing and turning
color from nature's touch. Everywhere they looked
they found broken, old weaponry. They were too
late to find the Armenian army which had survived
them for so long.

Samel's only encampment – a small makeshift
home with a bed suited for two.

Two Figs

While Çatli had been at war with Turkish soldiers, Alexander returned to Yozgat, dressed in his Ottoman uniform, and began finding lost and abducted children and women. He brought them to Turkish homes who were eager to help save the Armenians from the genocide and hide them until Alexander could bring them out of Yozgat at a more peaceful time.

While searching for his family, Alexander found his little nephew in the forest near Saray Köy.

A young Armenian wife and husband drive their car though the streets of southern France. The war in Europe was over for a time, and a life atop a mountain was now the past. They drove to their apartment on a sunny afternoon and stop for pedestrians. A car approaches and lingers perfectly beside theirs. A man holds a gun to Samel's head.

"Give me your money!" the man shouts. Çatli hands his wallet, and the thief drives off. The couple looks to each other and begin to laugh with relief.

About the Author

Aris Govjian is a writer and entrepreneur. He enjoys writing fiction as well as historical and philosophical nonfiction. Aris has been a lifelong supporter of various charities and causes, more specifically providing support to impoverished families and children in Armenia.

The author is the great great-grandson of the Aris Govjian mentioned in the story Spirits on the Mountain.

CPSIA information can be obtained
at www.ICGtesting.com
Printed in the USA
LVHW051049211120
672146LV00006B/854